CCSS Genre Folktale

M000189549

Essential Question
When has a plan helped you accomplish a task?

The
Riddle
of the Drum

A Tale from Mexico

by Ali MacKisack
illustrated by Janet Nelson

A Riddle and a Drum

A long time ago, in Mexico, there was a clever, resourceful, and beautiful princess who was of the marrying age. Being clever, resourceful, and beautiful, the princess didn't want to marry just any man. She wanted to marry someone who was clever, resourceful, and charming.

The princess's father loved her very much. He wanted the man she married to prove himself worthy of his daughter. He also wanted him to be a strong leader who could someday rule his kingdom.

The king hatched a plan to find a suitable husband for the princess. He would create a riddle. Whoever was able to solve the riddle would be allowed to ask for his daughter's hand in marriage.

The man who was able to solve the riddle would need to be capable and confident. He would also need persistence and planning. The king thought that a capable, confident man who could see a plan through would be just the right kind of man for his daughter. It would be up to her to decide if he was charming.

So the king had a drum made, but the drum was no ordinary drum. The head of the drum was as black as night and as shiny as a beetle's back. When the drum was struck, the hills all around echoed and boomed with a deep, rolling sound that had never been heard before. When the drum was played on the mountaintop, its sound rolled out across the land. Everyone knew it was the drum the king had made to test his daughter's suitors.

The king had his drummer walk though the streets of every town and every city in the land, playing the drum and calling:

Rat a tat tat, rumma tum tum
What is it made of
The head of this drum?

If you answer the riddle
Then you'll win the hand
Of the fairest princess in all
of this land.

Rat a tat tat, rumma tum tum
Can you guess the outcome?
Will you be the one?

Now, in a far corner of that country, there lived a prince who was also of the marrying age. The prince saw the king's drummer, listened to the strange rolling sound, and thought about the riddle of the drum.

The prince had heard of the cleverness, resourcefulness, and beauty of the king's daughter. He also realized that the king would not give up his daughter easily, so he knew that the riddle would be difficult. Despite this, the prince wanted to take up the challenge and marry the princess. He began to wonder how he might go about solving the riddle of the drum.

This prince was clever, and this prince was charming. He was also capable and confident. All that he needed now was a plan.

The prince thought and thought. He sought guidance from those around him. Sadly, the wise ones in his palace did not care for riddles and were of no use to him. So he thought some more. Then one day, he announced his plan to his brother.

"I don't know what skills I will need or what talents will be useful in my pursuit, so I will set out on this journey alone. Along the way, I will gather around me those with special skills—skills that may be useful for solving the riddle of the drum. By surrounding myself with talented people, I hope to solve the riddle and win the hand of the princess."

CHAPTER TWO

The Riddle Unfolds

And so the prince set off. It wasn't long before he saw a man on the road ahead of him. The man came toward him with amazing speed. Right away, the prince saw that here was a man with a special talent that might be useful to him.

The prince stopped the man and asked him his name.

"People call me the Runner," the man replied, "for I can run as fast as the wind."

"I am going to the palace to solve the riddle of the drum," the prince told the Runner. "Will you come, too, and help me?"

"I will come with you," said the Runner, and off they went together toward the palace.

Along the way, they met a man sitting by a river. The man was throwing stones across the water, and every stone he threw landed on the previous one. The prince was amazed to see a small tower emerging from the stones on the riverbank. The man was building the tower, stone by stone, so skilled was he at throwing.

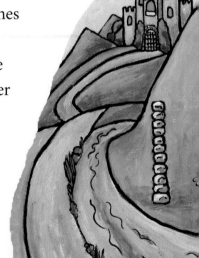

"I am going to the palace to solve the riddle of the drum," he told the Thrower. "Will you help me, too?"

"I will come with you," said the Thrower, and so off they went together toward the palace.

Next, they came upon a man who was lying with his ear pressed to the road. "Whatever are you doing?" asked the prince.

"I am listening to a conversation in the next town," said the Hearer. "They are saying that another man has just returned, defeated, for he, too, was unable to solve the riddle of the drum and marry the king's daughter."

"Solving the riddle is what I plan to do myself," said the prince. "Do you know what the answer is?"

"I do not know the right answer, but I can tell you what the wrong answers have been," said the Hearer. "From what I've heard, the drum is NOT made from—" and he started chanting:

The hide of a goat
Or the hide of a deer
The hide of a rabbit
Or the hide of a hare.
Nor is it the hide
Of a duck or a cow
A snake or a lizard
A toad or a sow.

"What a wonderful skill," thought the prince. He invited the Hearer to join him, assuring him that he would be rewarded if he could help to solve the riddle.

On the way to the palace, the prince gathered to him two more men with special talents. One was the Blower, who could whip up a windstorm by simply puffing out his cheeks. The other was the Eater. The Eater was a tiny man, but he could eat an entire cartload of food in just one sitting. The prince knew that the Eater could be costly to care for, and he didn't know how his skill might be useful. Despite this, the prince invited him to come along, too.

In time, the prince, the Runner, the Thrower, the Hearer, the Blower, and the Eater arrived at the palace gates. The Hearer put his ear to the ground.

"Look, Father," he heard the princess say. "Here comes a man who looks as if he has a plan, for he brings with him not one, but five others."

"Well, he might have a plan and five other men, but he will also need some luck," replied the king. "Who in the world could easily guess that I had the drum made from the hide of a very large flea?"

The Hearer stood up and smiled at the prince. "Here is the answer you need," he said, and he whispered into the prince's ear.

Early the next morning, the prince put on his best clothes and presented himself before the king and the princess. The prince's confident bearing impressed the king. The princess also liked what she saw.

They took the prince and his men to the place where the drum was kept. Then the drummer banged upon the drum. All around them, the hills echoed and boomed with a deep rolling sound. The prince listened carefully. Then he ran his hand thoughtfully over the shiny black skin of the drum.

"It seems to me," he said slowly, "that this drum is made from the hide of a very large flea."

The king gasped. The princess smiled. The prince smiled back. Then the king spoke again. "Very well," he said. "You have answered the riddle correctly. However, there are two more tasks that must be completed before any wedding may take place."

The king wanted to test the prince further, to make sure that he was truly worthy of his daughter.

That night, the prince was worried. "You have helped me so far," he said to his men, "and I thank you. However, now the king wants to test me again. I do not know what these tests will be. I do not know what we will be called upon to do. Let me assure you that if I'm successful and I marry the princess, I will reward you. You will live in comfort and style for the rest of your days."

The Final Tests

The next day, the king and the princess met them at the top of a very tall tower, which had a view for many miles, all the way across to the ocean.

"Send one of your men to the ocean to fill a bottle of water," the king instructed, "and I will send one of my servants, too. If my servant returns first, you may not ask for my daughter's hand." The Runner stepped up.

"I will run for the prince," he said, and the prince smiled at him in gratitude.

So the runners set off, covering the many miles toward the ocean. The Runner quickly realized that the woman he was racing against had special talents of her own. Once she had built up speed, she suddenly began leaping from the ground and flying short distances! Yet, even with her special skills, she wasn't as fast as the Runner, and he was soon far ahead.

He reached the ocean, filled his bottle, and was heading back to the tower before the woman was even halfway to the water. Ahead of him he saw a shady tree that beckoned, and he decided to rest for a few moments, for he was hot and very tired. Try as he might, he couldn't help but nod off. Before he knew it, he was fast asleep. The woman began to close the gap between them.

Outside the castle gates, the Hearer heard the Runner snoring and guessed what had happened.

"Quickly!" the Hearer said to the Thrower. "You must wake him before the woman gets to the tree." Just as the woman reached the tree, the Thrower threw a stone. Thwack! The stone split a branch from the tree, causing it to fall beside the Runner and wake him.

The Runner jumped up, but the woman was now ahead of him, running fast, and leaping into bursts of flight.

"Quickly!" the Hearer said to the Blower when he detected the sound of the woman's rapid approach. "Stop her from reaching the castle before the Runner."

So the Blower puffed up his cheeks. Every time the woman leapt from the ground, he blew up a windstorm that sent her flying back toward the tree.

High in his tower, the king looked on, puzzled at how his runner appeared to be running, yet was traveling backward. Little by little, the Runner gained ground. Before long, he appeared at the gates of the castle, ahead of the woman.

Soon after, the king met with the prince. "Very well. You have successfully completed that task," the king said. "One final task awaits you."

That night, the king invited the prince and his men to a banquet. The banquet hall was set up with two long tables, each stretching the length of the hall.

At one table sat the king's family and attendants, more than 100 people in all. At the other table were six chairs, one for the prince and each of his men. Yet, on each table there was the same quantity of food. The legs of the tables groaned beneath the weight of it.

"The man who marries my daughter must know how to feast and be merry," said the king. "My people will empty this table of food, and your people must do the same. If there is so much as a crumb of food left from the feast tonight, you may not ask for my daughter's hand in marriage."

The prince looked at the king's daughter, and she smiled at him. Then the prince looked at the Eater. The Eater smiled at the food. "Let us begin!" he said. Before the food on the table for the 100 people was half-gone, the prince's table had finished their feast.

Late that evening, the king addressed the crowd.

"This prince has won the right to marry my daughter," he proclaimed. "He has completed all the tasks I set for him and his men."

The king continued, "In doing so, he has shown that he can make a plan and be persistent. He has shown that he is capable and confident. In this way, he has proven that he is worthy of my daughter. Should my precious daughter wish to marry this man, then I shall give them my blessing."

Then the prince stepped up and took the princess's hand. "Will you marry me?" asked the prince. "Yes!" she replied. The crowd leaped to their feet, cheering and clapping. The prince couldn't wait to start planning the wedding. He also wondered what ideas his helpers might have for such a magnificent occasion.

Respond to Reading

Summarize

Use the most important details from *The Riddle of the Drum* to summarize how the prince's plan helped him win the princess. Your graphic organizer may help you.

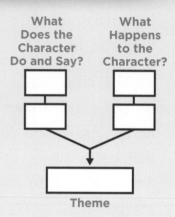

Text Evidence

1. How do you know that *The Riddle of the Drum* is a folktale? Give details from the story. **GENRE**

2. What is the theme of *The Riddle of the Drum*? How does the prince's successful plan support that message? **THEME**

3. Explain why "a shady tree that beckoned" on page 11 is an example of personification. **PERSONIFICATION**

4. Write about how the prince's plan helped the Runner obtain water from the ocean first. Tell how this helps communicate the theme. **WRITE ABOUT READING**

Compare Texts

Read about how a plan can help you make a drum.

Make a Drum

In the folktale *The Riddle of the Drum*, the king has a drum made from the hide of a very large flea. You might not be able to find a very large flea in your neighborhood, but you can probably find all the materials you need to make your own drum.

What you need

- large tin can, such as a baby formula or coffee can
- wrapping paper, cut-out pictures, or fabric to cover the outside of your drum
- some thin rope or yarn
- rubber inner tube to make the skin of the drum (Ask at a tire shop or garden store.)
- hole punch
- strong craft glue
- scissors

Step 1.

Wash and dry the can and the rubber inner tube.

Step 2.

Cut the paper, pictures, or fabric to match the size of your can.

Step 3.

Glue the paper, pictures, or fabric around the outside of the can.

Step 4.

Cut out two circles from the inner tubes. They need to be at least two inches larger than the diameter of the can.

Step 5.

Ask an adult to help you punch holes at regular intervals around the outer edge of each rubber circle—about eight holes per circle.

Step 6.

Put one rubber circle on the table and center the can on top of it. Next, center the other rubber circle on top of the can.

Step 7.

Thread one end of the rope or yarn through a hole in the bottom rubber circle, knotting it on the outside. Pull it up through a hole in the top rubber circle, and continue zigzagging your way around the rest of the drum.

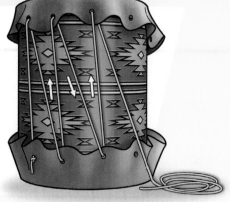

Step 8.

Adjust the rope so that the top and bottom rubber circles are evenly stretched over the ends of the can. A tighter "skin" will make a better sound.

Step 9.

When you are happy with the stretch in your rubber circles, knot the rope and make a holding strap from the remaining rope or yarn.

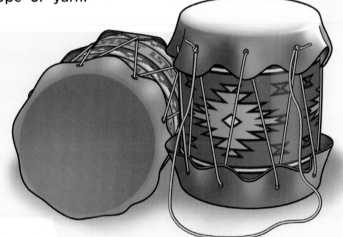

Step 10.

Bang your drum!

Make Connections

How does having numbered steps help you to make a drum? **ESSENTIAL QUESTION**

How is the prince's plan in *The Riddle of the Drum* similar to the instructions in *Make a Drum*?

TEXT TO TEXT

Illustration: Martin Simpson

Focus on

Genre

Folktale Folktales are short stories that come from a spoken storytelling tradition. In most folktales a character has to complete a challenge or solve a riddle to win a reward. The characters may have special powers, abilities, or friends who help them.

Read and Find

- *The Riddle of the Drum* begins with the phrase "A long time ago," suggesting it is an old, traditional tale (page 2).

- The king creates a riddle to find the best husband for his beautiful daughter. He has a drum made out of the hide of a very large flea, which no one would think to guess (page 9).

- The prince outsmarts the king by using his own men's special powers or abilities—those of the Runner, Hearer, Thrower, Blower, and Eater (pages 11–14).

Your Turn

Think of another challenge the king might set for the prince. Describe the plan the prince would need to ensure he could win the challenge, using the help of his friends and their special powers.